## SUMMER MORN...WINTER WEATHER

POEMS 'TWIXT HAIKU AND SENRYU

Youth like summer morn,
age like winter weather...

SHAKESPEARE, *The Passionate Pilgrim*

*Other books by the author*

THE ETERNAL SOLITARY: A Study of Joseph Conrad

SELECTED POEMS AND TRANSLATIONS

CUP OF FURY, a novel

INTRODUCTION TO MODERN POLISH LITERATURE (with Ludwik Krzyżanowski)

CONTEMPORARY ISRAELI LITERATURE

THE DANCING SOCRATES AND OTHER POEMS OF JULIAN TUWIM

POEMS OF THE GHETTO: A TESTAMENT OF LOST MEN

IN THE MANNER OF HAIKU: Seven Aspects of Man

DAILY NEW AND OLD: Poems in the Manner of Haiku

STRANGE MUTATIONS: Poems in the Manner of Haiku

CONRAD AND SHAKESPEARE and Other Essays

JOSEPH CONRAD: COMMEMORATIVE ESSAYS (with Ludwik Krzyżanowski)

# SUMMER MORN...
# WINTER WEATHER

POEMS 'TWIXT HAIKU AND SENRYU

### by
### Adam Gillon

*art work by*

ALICE D. PHALEN

ASTRA BOOKS • NEW YORK

*Copyright* © 1976 by Adam Gillon

ALL RIGHTS RESERVED

Library of Congress Catalog
Card Number 75-38484
ISBN....0-913994-23-5

ASTRA BOOKS, NEW YORK

Order Department
Box 392, Times Square Station
New York, N.Y. 10036

Editorial Offices
369 Lexington Ave., Suite 906
New York, N.Y. 10017
(212) 986-1359

PRINTED IN THE UNITED STATES OF AMERICA

**for Iris**

## Acknowledgment

I wish to thank my friend Alfred H. Marks for his criticism and valuable suggestions.

A.G.

## CONTENTS

FOREWORD 9

I
GREAT CREATING NATURE 11

II
A LOCAL HABITATION AND A NAME 61

III
QUINTESSENCE OF DUST 87

IV
THIS WIDE GAP OF TIME 137

## FOREWORD

let the meaning
echo before
and after

*haiku* — the seasons
merely a keen moment of
perceiving nature

in *senryu* the world
as it's now — critical view
of human nature

together they tell
the real poetical
nature of life

There is an art which in their piedness shares
With great creating nature.

SHAKESPEARE, *The Winter's Tale*

# I
# GREAT CREATING NATURE

**Summer Day**

early summer morn
boy rushes out to see
how the day is born

calling his dog
the boy running to the lake
ah, the freshness

boy on a beach
caresses a stone
smoothed by the sea

bullfrog printed
into macadam by
motor vehicle




ignoring car horns
slowing shaking its head
turtle crossing street




motorists swerve
to avoid hitting
skunk's smelly carcass

chain saw
silenced by louder
crows' caw




summer breeze
dissolves the morning haze
rustling the trees

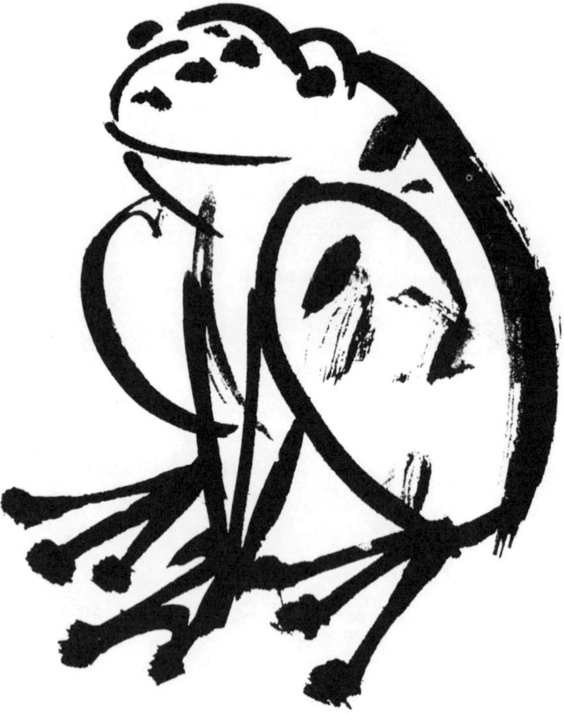

    huge
    toad

               frozen

                             at
                             water's
                             edge

iguana
immured

    one
    with
    black
    granite

        suddenly
        breaks
        free

black
horsefly
captured

    shaking
    invisible

        web
        of
        spider

hawk
cruising
aloft

      my
      eyes
      scan
      the
      ground
      seeking

            the
            prey
            he
            will
            strike

butterfly

    ends
    its
    flight
    colliding

        with
        my
        car's
        headlight

shimmering balloon
floating over the trees —
full summer moon

**Autumn Rain**

not a single star
stopping at the curb
splashed by car




pouring rain
the old streetwalker
cries out in pain

outseasoned:
katytid slowly rasps
his own requiem

clouds in autumn sky—
below a cruising hawk and
monarch butterfly




under the white pine
a slippery circle
of brown needles

**Birches**

slender birch trees
    distant cousins
        of bamboos


white birches bend low
    pay homage to the wind
        then swing back sighing


black snake
    coiled on birch trunk
        part of its pattern

    duck seeking shelter
        ashore near frozen pond —
            now bones and feathers


    cold morning: cars crawl
        huddle on the expressway
            trying to get warm

bread crumbs on the snow
    bring a host of chattering
        sparrows, chickadees

sunny winter day
    flies buzz on window panes —
        unwelcome late guests

glowing fireplace
      dog and I motionless —
    winter fellowship

shells
on
mantelpiece

        sounds
        of
        the
        sea

                catching
                fire

storing winter clothes
in camphor-filled closet
letting out the spring

wild geese land on pond
awakening the farmer
with their loud cries

birds
hid
in
flue

        protest

                the
                sudden
                fire

bird's
　　shadow

　　　　　dances
　　　　　merrily

　　　　　　　　on
　　　　　　　　sunlit
　　　　　　　　roof

red poppies growing
in this blood-soaked field muffle
the groans of the dying

intricate plane —
    a menace to nature's
        intricate balance

. . . as imagination bodies forth
The forms of things unknown, the poet's pen
Turns them to shapes, and gives to airy nothing
A local habitation and a name.

SHAKESPEARE, *A Midsummer-Night's Dream*

# II
# A LOCAL HABITATION AND A NAME

## BORGUND, NORWAY

In Borgund stave church
    reindeer horns bleach
        under a cobweb

**Kyoto, Japan**

every man
    has his own
        Kyoto

**Teheran, Iran**

Crown Jewels Museum
outside blind beggar's plate
with copper coins

**Bathhouse, Bankok, Thailand**

marked by number plates
young women wait to be bought
out of the glass cage

**Haiti**

boy in a rowboat
below the ocean liner
diving for coins

**Israel, Masada**

brown bushes
in the Judean desert —
life in arid expanse



singing tourists
in cable car swinging over
silent Masada

**New York City**


   across the sky's blackboard
      the jet's signature
         in white




   the clatter of cans
      thrown by garbage collectors
     wakes the city




   in crowded Times Square
     a violinist performs
        while passersby stare

   sizzling summer day
      broiled ducks strung in window
         Chinatown shop display




   rush hour —
      the subway empties
         its swirling bowels




   in a singles' bar
      aging woman pretending
         she's a big star

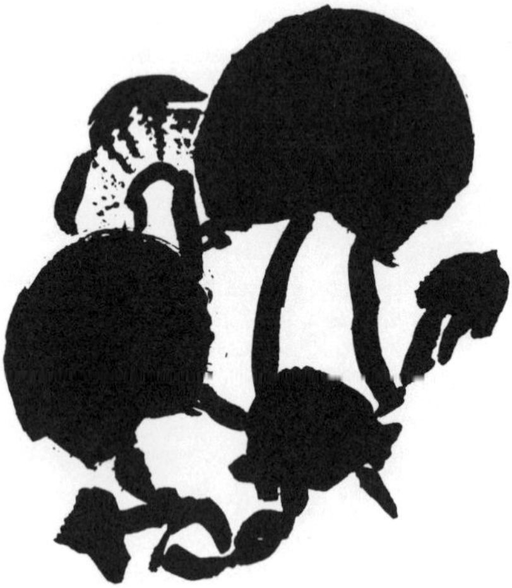

**GRAFFITI**

unlettered
youngsters

    deface
    the
    city

        with
        fancy
        lettering

**Woodstock Festival, New York**

six-hundred thousand
huddled shoulder to shoulder—
and no one killing

barefoot ragged youth
driving red convertible
to a rock concert


**Rt. 80, California**

a plastic horse
riding on top of a sign:
motor lodge

**Gardiner, New York**

on a wind-swept hill
a richness of flowers
and a run-down shack



stiff deer hanging from
a stately oak branch—below
beer-guzzling hunters



the deer watches me
I gaze at him from the car
stalled by his stillness

**Muir Woods National Monument, California**

tilting my head back
    to view the giant redwood tree
        I feel I'm a dwarf

the size of a tree
    is no indication —
        of its true age

the age of man
    is no indication
        of his wisdom

**Fishermen's Wharf, San Francisco**

around the former
    prison of Alcatraz Isle
        white sails soar freely


seagull alights
    on white lamp post
        as the light goes on


a $10 bill
    separates Lobster Thermidor
        from fish 'n chips

**La Jolla, California**

at La Jolla beach
a fully clad man gazes
at naked bathers

**Las Vegas, Nevada**

woman feeding quarters
with closed eyes to
blinking slot machine

**Main Street, USA**

Eat'n'shop then bank
offices churches churches
funeral parlors

**Acapulco, Mexico**

armed soldier band
startling tourists and peddlers—
black boots on the sand

**The Alps, Switzerland**

tourist viewing
panoramic mountain top:
"Pretty like a picture!"

**Atlantic Ocean**

ocean liner queen
leaving in her churning wake
a trail of refuse

And yet to me what is this
quintessence of dust? Man delights not
me—no, nor woman neither...

SHAKESPEARE, *Hamlet*

# III

# QUINTESSENCE OF DUST

**Ceasing to Grow**

  when a tree ceases
     to grow it is still a tree
        burning wood




  when your mind ceases
     to grow you're decaying flesh
        merely burning food

**Music**

without the player
the piano is a useless
piece of furniture




woman and violin
her body another
silent instrument

music lover
assisting orchestra
with drumming fingers




explaining music with words—
as futile as explaining
poetry with music




synthetic music
sprayed over majestic
silence of mountain

**Lovemaking**

after
lovemaking

    she
    sits
    naked
    on
    bed

        watching
        him
        dress

**Illusion**

she
fell
in
love
with

        a
        resonant
        sexy
        voice

                and
                then
                she
                saw
                him

**Escape**

enduring the anguish
of a borrowed life actor
forgets his own pain

graduate trying
to balance mortar board
on an Afro cut

**Cigarettes**

    cigarette ad
        follows official warning
            against smoking

    reading the sign NO SMOKING
        and lighting his cigarette

**Patience**

    whether patients die
        or get well—their doctor will
            get well-to-do

**Dying**

sick man works hard
    at office and home
        trying to cheat death



his rank and wealth
    can't stop the progress of
        terminal cancer



doctor saves one
    twenty-week-old baby
        aborts another

**Murderers and Victims**


child killer
    not punished being
        a child himself

alleged murderer
    arraigned for trial
        victim not alleged

a million dollars
    to try sadistic killer—
        nothing for the victim

**Communication**

cocktail party
    everybody speaks at once—
        nobody listens


with all the media
    inarticulate youngsters
        like man like you know

**Food For Thought**

TV dinner—
    watching scenes of starvation
        in Bangla-Desh




**Terrorism**

innocent humans
    tortured slaughtered and maimed
        for humane causes

**The Evening News**

after report of
disastrous train derailment
a singing commercial

### Media
### Bicentennial Bargain

SUPER GREAT GO LIE
FABULOUS EXTRA FUN SAIL
SPECTACULAR BUY

SEND NOW TAKE A PILL
LIMITED OFFER STEAL SALE
BARGAIN VALUE KILL

PAY ONLY ONE BILL
DONT MISS YOUR CHANCE DONT FAIL
GROW RICH NOW HOLD STILL

EAT SMOKE SIP DRINK DIE
JOIN ME NOW FLY ME FLY GAIL
DISCOUNT HOPE BUY BUY

**Politics**

congressman goes to
    Washington to ensure his
        return to Congress




in the Promised Land
    politicians no longer
        promise anything

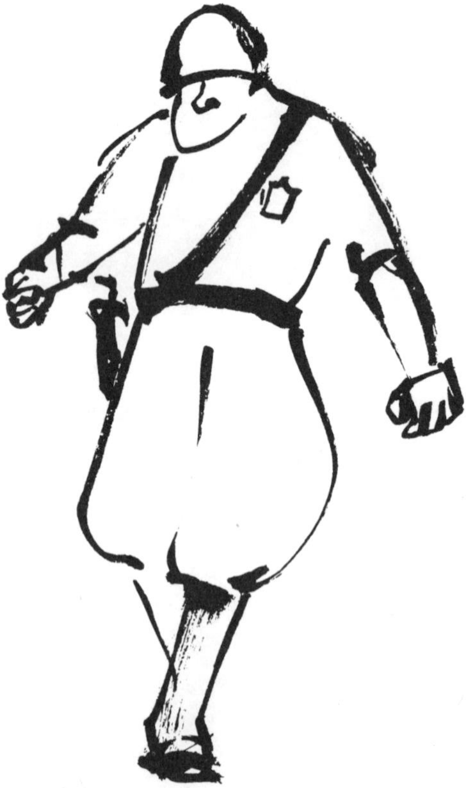

**Authority**

traffic
cop
slowly

        strides
        towards
        car

                of
                speeder

bureaucrat
late

      fumbling
      with
      papers

            while
            people
            wait

    this unbeliever
        zealously upholds
           his creed










                suspect the man
                    who condemns lust
                      too lustily

**People's Democracy**

Dictator's order:
    "The people are the master.
     I am your servant!"


**Dreams and History**

dreamers make history
   but history defies
      the visions of dreamers

**The Good Wife**

"My husband knows best."
then she proceeds to run things
as she knows best


**Women's Lib**

she won the power
in the marketplace but lost
her woman's power



her liberated
sexuality
makes him impotent

**Losing Weight**

obese customer
worked over
by slim masseur


**Thrift**

cleaning up drawer
of accumulated junk
he puts some things back

**Cages**

    gigantic bird cage
        gives lots of room for flight
      but no freedom




    in the monkey cage
        the human observer takes
      a look at himself

**The Samaritan**

bending over dog
    he has run over, the boy
        killed by another car

**Progress**

aerosol cans and
    supersonic airplanes —
        soon no air at all

Lead us from hence, where we may leisurely
Each one demand and answer to his part
Performed in this wide gap of time...

SHAKESPEARE, *The Winter's Tale*

# IV

# THIS WIDE GAP OF TIME

**Children**

"I'll run away."
    young girl threatens mother —
        time runs out for both




When past and future blend:
    Old man's "I remember *when*..."
        Child's "*When* I grow up..."




nurtured in freedom
    young man cannot value it —
        he needs tyranny

**Parents**

   protective parents
       protected their child
           right into his grave




   abusive parents
       pummelling children
           to ease their own pain




   It is ten p.m.
       Do you know
           where your parents are?

**Aspects of Youth**


fire-spitting dragsters
chase the end of the rainbow
and big prize money




Power to the workers!
demands militant student
who has never worked




protesting the war
pacifist students go on a
violent rampage

**Aspects of Age**

this old photograph
    poignant reminder of what
        he no longer is


watching his old dog,
    listening to its labored breath
        he feels his own age


dreaming of youth
    the old man has forgotten
        young man's misery

**Aspects of Age**

the aging man looks
with wonder and nostalgia
at young girl's firm breast




middle-aged lover
wants his young mistress in bed —
she prefers night clubs




old crone rummaging
in garbage can, cuts piece off
old musty carpet

**Elegy**

    page hand-written by
the son he lost years ago —
    live voice from the past

    telling his son tales
of past perils—unaware
of son's perilous future

    he rejected life
to celebrate a proper
    manner of living

    twenty years
searching for life's meaning—
he found it in death

    renouncing his life
he leaves a note which lives
    in his father's mind

    he puts on the shirt
recalling his son wore it
    on the day he died

    in God's time-ledger
twenty years or seventy—
    only a second

death's gnawing sorrow
   life renews itself—
      life's marrow


do not lament death
   it is only a pause in
      life's eternal breath


seeking for daylight
   you dream of eternity—
      you wake up—it's night


most eloquent utterance
   of the universe —
      universal silence


shattered worlds
explode into cosmic dust—
   then new worlds

to
comprehend
infinity

    you
    need

        an
        infinite
        life

neither past nor future
the moment is all we have —
the NOW the I AM




let each day count
as if it were
the last day

## Poetry Books by Adam Gillon

### *The Dancing Socrates and other Poems by Julian Tuwim*

Selected and Translated with an Introduction by ADAM GILLON.
Julian Tuwim (1894-1953) is generally regarded as one of Poland's greatest modern poets. Cloth $6.00
Distributed by TWAYNE PUBLISHERS—A Division of G. K. Hall & Co., Boston, Mass.

### *Poems of the Ghetto a testament of lost men*

This anthology ranges from poems written in the seclusion of a writer's study to those composed shortly before the author's death—in the stench of the concentration camp, the cellar, or even in the death van.

"The ghetto poets offered grimly lucid pictures of shattered lives and hopes. But their stanzas were also the magic potion which occasionally restored a moment of clarity and peace to the tortured mind. . ."
—*From the Introduction*
Illustrated by Si Lewen   Cloth: $6.00

### DAILY NEW AND OLD
*poems in the manner of haiku*

Shakespeare's utterances on the seasons of life are used as a framework for the author's commentary on nature, personal loss, youthful love and self-destruction, and the baffling manifestations of the contemporary human condition. The three parts form one thematic unit whose tonality is lyrical, elegaic or satirical.

The art work by Haig Shekerjian is based on original Japanese paintings and calligraphy.   Cloth: $4.50 Paper: $2.50


## SELECTED POEMS AND TRANSLATIONS

Dr. Gillon . . . has collected in this handsomely produced volume a number of his own original poems as well as his poetic renderings from Russian, Polish and Hebrew . . . truly poetic recreations of the original poems. The scant body of artistic English verse translation from the Polish has been considerably increased by this collection.

LUDWIK KRZYZANOWSKI
*The Polish Review, N.Y.*


"Regret at the loss of Dr. Gillon to New York State University College is deepened by the range and quality of his latest book of verse. Of the 45 poems in this volume, 21 are attractive verse translations from Russian, Polish and Hebrew. The remaining 24 are original expressions of poetic sensibility, usually expressed in free verse."

**WATSON KIRKCONNELL**
*President, Acadia University*
Cloth: $4.50

### IN THE MANNER OF HAIKU:
*seven aspects of man*

In these poems, the theme is human behavior in its fascinating variety. Some of the epigrammatic pieces reveal the paradoxes of modern life; others are in a lighter vein. Line drawings by Mary Jane Harley add a visual dimension which perfectly recaptures the spirit of the poetry.

"Bravo for *In the manner of haiku!* Delightful, original, cuts to the bone!"
Eric W. Amann, *Editor, HAIKU*
(144 pages illustrated)
Cloth: $4.50 Paper: $2.50


### STRANGE MUTATIONS
*in the manner of haiku*

Carefully selected Shakespearean quotations provide a framework for the strange mutations Gillon observes in man and nature. The changing seasons, the contrasts between youth and age, the harmony and the discordant notes of human existence are explored with poignant beauty. Haig Shekerjian's startling illustrations lend felicitous emphasis to the text.   Paper $2.50 Cloth $4.50

# Review of *The Dancing Socrates*

"In *The Dancing Socrates* he has performed a feat that is rare indeed—he has made himself disappear. Dr. Gillon has achieved that *magnum desideratum* of all great translators (and there is such a thing as a great translator—*vide* Edward Fitzgerald of *Rubaiyat* fame); he has made himself invisible to the reader. This extraordinary feat has been accomplished but rarely since the forty English churchmen worked together for four years on the King James Version of the Bible in the dawning of the seventeenth century...

"In addition to the intricacies of transmitting poetry from one language to another, Dr. Gillon transmits Tuwim's thought from his *first* language (a la Joseph Conrad) Polish, into his *third* language (also a la Conrad), English. Both the poet and the translator have also worked considerably in Russian, which makes Gillon's affinity for the right phrase, the correct, astute reading of Tuwim more easily understandable. This unerring ear for the proper note was tuned by the same words heard from childhood by both poets, translator and translated...

"Every poem in the collection is a tribute to both poets, so far apart in space and time, and yet so near in meter and rhyme.

"In this golden anniversary year of the publication of *Sokrates Tańczący*, it is good to have available Dr. Gillon's sensitive rendition of *The Dancing Socrates*, and everyone interested in the progress of Polish poetic expression and culture should offer a vote of confidence and thanks by reading and cherishing this little book."

EDMUND A. BOJARSKI
*McMurry College*
*Founding Editor, Conradiana*

# Reviews of *Poems of the Ghetto*

"An olive on muted green wrapper covers and eerie black on white prints accompany Professor Gillon's translations of Polish ghetto poems. The presence of the writers who experienced the ghetto and of those who escaped Nazi camp horrors overshadows the cover and the prints. Perhaps neither Jews nor Gentiles have been able to internalize knowledge of Nazi Germany's attempted genocide of the Jewish People. . . .

"Because we may never be able to hold onto the palpable reality of the tragic immolation to insanity of six million individual human beings and because we must, Gillon's anthology is crucial reading. . .

"Too many contemporary poets write insipid lines that underline a dearth of talent and emotional experience; they fail to offer qualitative art to a flesh-and-blood audience. . .

"Readers who are impatient with pseudo-poetic word games or insults to your emotional, intellectual, and aesthetic sensibilities: turn to Adam Gillon's translations of ghetto poems. Many of the images are permanent; the rhythms are of life-in-death.
  Read.
  This is our history.
  This is what I read to the dead. . .(Władysław Szlengel,
   p. 62.)"
  *University of North Carolina at Greensboro*  MARIAN STEIN
                   *The Polish Review*

"Shot through Gillon's book is the darkness; but there is also the faith of a resurrection morning. . . . .For every word Jesus cried from the cross, another Jew in this book lived. 'O Christ, crucified on bloody Polish roads, driven by hate from the threshold of the church, where is thy place in these times of crime and dread?' "

                   CHRIS FARLEKAS
                 *The Times Herald Record*